MANIFEST YOUR POWER

HOW TO REALIZE YOUR DREAMS AND LIVE THE LIFE YOU DESIRE

ALISON DAVIES

ILLUSTRATIONS BY KELLI LADERER

Hardie Grant

QUADRILLE

Consider your life right now. What would you like to attract more than anything? A new relationship, your dream job or to save enough money to one day have your own place? Perhaps you don't yet know what you're looking for and need to clarify your true purpose and find a way to move forwards – our needs and requirements change on a daily basis, and so do our goals. Some objectives have a short life span, while others are more long term, but with the right manifestation techniques, we can work towards both kinds of aims. We are all in control of our destiny, even if we don't realize it. All it takes is a little imagination, focus and persistence.

Manifestation is based on one of the main principles of the universe: like attracts like. Everything is made up of energy, so if we want to attract something into our life, we need to match that energy and focus on it every day. It's a simple equation: ask, believe and you will receive. This combined with tools and other techniques – such as using vision boards, scripts and positive affirmations – can take you a long way to achieving your goal.

Once you begin your journey and start manifesting the things you want, you'll realize that the power lies with you. How you think and feel plays a big part in the reality that you create. For example, when you start the day feeling positive, looking forward to each moment and visualizing it in your mind, then each task you face becomes more joyful and the day goes smoothly. If you dread the day ahead, then you will carry that mindset with you like a cloud above your shoulders and little tasks will become much bigger and more of struggle.

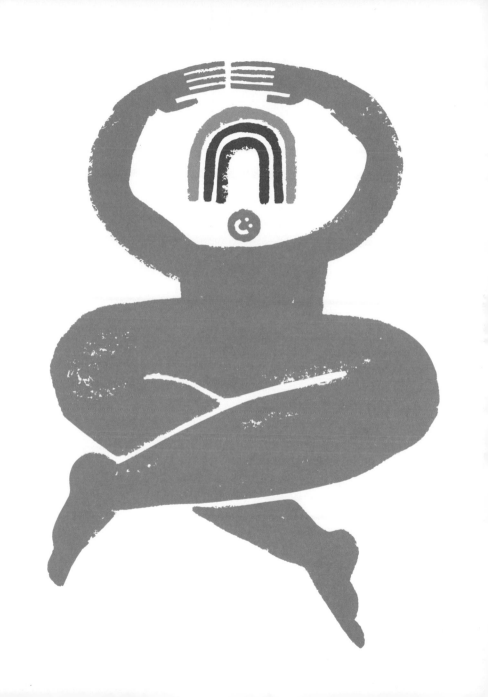

Of course, you'll still face challenges and setbacks because that's life, but once you realize that you have the ability to attract anything you want, you'll feel empowered and able to deal with life's ups and downs. You'll even be grateful for those downs and the lessons that they bring.

This book looks at the power of manifestation and how you can use simple tools to create the life you want. It gives you the essentials that you need to become a manifesting genius! Whether you're a complete beginner or you have a little knowledge that you want to put into practice, this book will show you where to start. You might have heard a bit about manifestation and feel intrigued, and that's okay. The step-by-step guidance, practical activities and suggestions you find within these pages will help you make sense of it all and could change your life. Even if you've had some experience of manifesting, you'll find out how to improve your chances of success and attract the positive energy you need to shape your future.

You'll learn how to identify what you want and what steps to take to attract it using a number of different tools. You'll also discover the power of vision boards, and how you can create one for any area of your life, from coming up with the original concept to using the board as a tool to help you find your focus. You'll learn what to include to make your vision board a success and the little tips and tricks that will give you the edge, and let the universe know that you're open and ready to receive the flow of abundance in your life.

Affirmations are also an important part of your toolkit, and you'll discover how to create the ones that work for you, and how to use them alongside your vision board and other techniques such as scripting, meditation and visualization. Tips on tracking your progress are also included, from celebrating successes to juggling short and long-term goals using different techniques.

Whether you're looking to expand your spiritual knowledge, dip your toe in the water with manifesting, or make some positive changes to your life and the world around you, this guide will give you the basics you need. Manifesting is a gift that will enhance your life. It doesn't matter what you want. It can be anything from material things, such as finding the perfect pair of jeans or a great new place to live, to the more practical, such as nailing that job interview – or even spiritual gifts like inner strength, balance and renewal. It's all there for the taking – all you have to do is ask and believe you have the power.

The Origins of Manifestation

Manifestation first emerged as part of the New Thought Philosophy, a spiritual movement founded in the US in the 19th century, although many of the core beliefs can also be found in spiritual practices and religions such as Hinduism and Buddhism. At its core is the idea that everything is made up of energy, including us, and we can work with this energy both for healing and to attract the things we want.

Rhonda Byrne's bestselling book *The Secret*, which was first published in 2006, went some way to bringing manifestation to the masses. The law of attraction, which underpins this book, is a key part of the manifestation process and works with the idea that if you think positively, you'll attract positive things. Since that time, the belief that you have the power to shape your own life using manifestation techniques has become increasingly popular worldwide.

How It Works

Manifestation is about turning your dreams into a reality, by switching up your mindset and using the power of positive thought. In other words, if you focus on your aspirations and think positively, you can work towards making them happen.

It sounds simple and it is up to a point, but it is not a one-sided process. You do have to put the work in and be prepared to take action to reach your goals. You can make a wish, but you need follow through and take the necessary steps to help things along.

Manifestation means collaborating with the universe and working together to create the life you want. It's about looking for those signs and clues and trusting your intuition. This is something that happens naturally when you're focused on a goal and in the right mindset. You become more aware of the opportunities around you, and you instinctively know which ones can help you turn your dream into a reality.

There is also an element of self-belief, of letting go and trusting that everything will work out, but this doesn't mean giving up on your goal and doing nothing. It's about finding a place of peace and balance. From here you will find it easier to recognize what is right for you, and what you need to do to create something wonderful.

Positive and Negative Thinking

One of the first steps in the manifestation process is being aware of your thoughts. Are you naturally a positive or a negative person? You might think this has nothing to do with what happens in your life, but it does affect the way you see things and deal with them. It shapes your mindset and your inner world. It colours your thoughts and what you focus on and this, in turn, shapes your reality.

Think of yourself as an artist. It is up to you to create the beautiful painting that is your life. Your thoughts are the ideas that you will paint upon the canvas. If they are bright and colourful, they will make the picture come to life, but if they are cloaked in shadow, they will create a much darker, less desirable portrait.

Your focus is also important. Where your attention lies is where you direct your energy, so if you're continually focused on a bad situation or something that you don't want to happen, you are actually feeding that narrative and are more likely to make it a reality. If you focus on a positive situation or story, then you're giving it the energy it needs to grow and come to fruition.

Understanding the Laws of the Universe

Manifestation takes practice; it doesn't happen overnight, although once you've perfected your skills and put everything in place, things can progress quickly. It's about understanding the process and some of the basic laws and principles. Once you understand how the universe works, you begin to work with it and that's when you'll see results.

Ancient civilizations spent a great deal of their time learning the secrets of the universe. They paid attention to the subtle shifts in energy and looked deeply into how the world worked. It's thought that they discovered a number of different laws, which we now call universal laws, that go some way to explaining how we can create and work with positive energy to attract what we need.

To help you on your journey here are some of the key universal laws and how they help with manifestation:

Like Attracts Like - the Law of Attraction
This is one of the most important laws of the universe and it plays a significant role in any manifesting technique. It means matching what you want with how you are, so if you want to attract positive things, then you need to have a positive outlook. If you want to attract money, then you need to have an attitude of abundance and give thanks for all the wonderful things you already have in your life right now. The energy we put out is exactly what we get back. You may have noticed this at work in your life already. It's a powerful truth and it works so well that sometimes we get more of the same back. This is why you should check in with yourself and know that you are sending out the right signals.

Raise Your Vibration - the Law of Energy

Think of yourself as a beacon of light. If you want to attract the universe's attention, then all you need to do is turn up your shine. Everything is made up of energy, which vibrates at different levels – and that includes you. When you're on top form, that energy is buzzing at a higher frequency, but when you're feeling under the weather, the vibration is much lower. You'll recognize the difference when you have a day where everything goes to plan and you're full of vitality. You'll be aware that you feel more alive and vibrant. This is because you've raised your energy vibration and the universe responds by sending you more of the same positive energy. When you manifest and your energy vibration is raised, you'll feel empowered and inspired. You'll set in motion a snowball effect as you attract more good things into your life.

Cause and Effect – the Law of Karma

You might have heard the saying 'what goes around comes around', and that's what this law is all about. When you go out of your way to do something good for someone, not only will you feel good but you're also building up positive karma. Think of it like a bank, but instead of dealing in currency, this bank looks after your karmic wealth and all of your good deeds. When you do something positive for someone else, you send a powerful message to the universe. You give back from the heart and this creates positive energy. You might not see the results of your efforts straight away but they are safe in the karmic bank. When the time is right and you're in the flow of manifestation, you'll start to see the rewards of all the karmic energy you've been saving up.

Believe and Breathe – the Law of Patience

In life, there is a time for everything; this is how the universe works. If the time is right, then it will happen; if it's not, then you can't force it. That doesn't mean that it won't happen but that it may take a little longer. Think about nature, the way it moves through different seasons in a never-ending cycle of transitions. You can't force the onset of spring when you're standing in the middle of winter; you have to allow the changes to come naturally.

Manifestation works with the power of the universe and the cycles of life. You may set your intention and think positive thoughts, but what you desire will only manifest when it is the right time for you. This might mean in a week, a month or even a year. Once you have put your request out there, it's important to take a step back, to breathe, relax and know that your wish is being actioned by the universe. Trust in the process and believe it will happen when the time is right.

Expect and You Will Receive – the Law of Expectation

Ever wondered why certain people are so successful? They seem to reach the top of their game with very little effort. In reality, they probably put a lot of work in behind the scenes but, most importantly, they never lose their self-belief. They expect to be a success and so they are. It's a simple equation. The universe responds to positive action and energy, so if you want your manifesting to work, you have to believe that it will. Whatever you wish for, you must wholeheartedly believe that you deserve it. Expect it to happen and act like it already has, then watch as it manifests before your eyes.

Take Inspired Action – the Law of Action

The universe might have the power to grant your wishes, but you have to do your bit too. Yes, manifesting is about expecting and receiving, but it's also about taking inspired action, being open to the universe and looking for the opportunities it opens to you that fit with your desired outcome. For example, you might want to find your own place and leave home. You set your intention, begin practising your preferred manifesting techniques and practise positive thinking, but you also need to be open and aware of signs and chance encounters. You might meet someone at college who introduces you to a friend who has a room in a shared house. At this point, an inspired action might be to have a coffee with this person and see if you get on, let them know of your interest and see what happens. The universe responds when you take positive action, and this is an important element of any type of manifesting.

As you work through the book, you will find that these laws will be part of everything you do, with perhaps one or other coming to the fore in different circumstances and when using different techniques.

- Do a mindful check of how you feel throughout the day. Stop and ask yourself whether your thoughts and feelings fit with what you want to manifest.

- Doing things you love naturally raises your energy vibration, so find some joy in everyday activities, whether you're laughing with a friend, being creative or simply pampering yourself. Do what feels good and turn up your shine.

- Being kind is one of the best ways to build good karma. A smile, a few words of encouragement, holding a door open for someone or a subtle gesture that makes someone's day a little bit better, like helping with chores, is enough to create positive energy.

- If you feel impatient, take a moment to focus on your breathing. Draw a deep breath in and count four slow beats then, as you exhale, do the same. Do not rush the process. Calm your mind by repeating this cycle of mindful breathing for a few minutes. Close your eyes and imagine what it will be like to have your goal come to fruition. How will you feel? Really connect with those emotions and bring them to the surface. Think, act and expect to receive.

- Make a list of positive actions that would help you reach your goal.

Set a Firm Foundation

Before you set out on a journey, you need to think about where you are going and why you want to go there. The journey to manifestation is no different and you will find all the guidance you need as you work through this book.

Identify Your Intention

The first and most important step to making your manifestation a success is to set a clear intention. Think of it like ordering a take-out. You might fancy a pizza but if you don't tell the restaurant what kind you'd like, then you can't complain if they don't bring your favourite. If you don't specify exactly what you want, then you won't get it, or you might get something similar but not what you intended.

It's easy to have an idea in mind, but if you're not clear on the details, this can cause chaos when manifesting. If it's something material that you want, then it's a simple case of stating exactly what you would like; for example, a gold halter neck dress is a clear enough statement, but when you're dealing with much broader needs – like a sense of peace and balance – then you need to go one step further and think about what this means to you. What would balance bring to your life? When you think of being at peace, what does this mean for you? Have a clear picture in your mind of what you need and why you need it so that the universe can deliver exactly what you ordered.

What's Your Motivation?

Manifestation is personal. It's about you and what you want and about making that happen in a way that suits you. Having defined what it is you want, you might be tempted to rush straight into asking for it, but it's important to take your time, reflect on where you are in your life, what you want for the future and why. Consider where you'd like to be in five years' time and think about the steps you need to take to get there. This will help you establish your current goals. Spend some time meditating and give yourself space to identify key areas that you'd like to work on, such as your education, career or relationships.

You don't have to try to manifest everything all at once; in fact, a step-by-step approach is often better. You can work on short-term goals, then plan out longer-term aspirations. There is no limit to the number of things you can manifest or how far into the future you can go.

Manifestation is a process, and it starts with your ability to identify your desire and why it's important to you. Remember to be specific and understand your motivation. For example, you might think you want to be a millionaire – and who wouldn't, right? But aside from the obvious, ask yourself why do you need more money in your life? Is it because you're not managing your finances and things feel out of control? If so, what you really crave is some order and balance. Perhaps you see money as security and you want more so that you feel safe and grounded. Or maybe you think money will give you the freedom to do the things you want to do.

There's nothing wrong with asking for abundance, but it's important to know what's behind this. Once you've uncovered the real motivation for your request, you can focus on this to help you manifest everything you need to make your goal a reality.

Start Where You Are Right Now

You now have a starting point, from which you can begin to manifest. You've identified your core motivations and intentions, and you'll learn to use a variety of techniques to manifest them as you go through this book. You can also take action by addressing any issues that might be holding you back.

The universe responds to positive thoughts and actions, so if you want more money but you're struggling to manage your finances, you can look at ways to keep on top of your accounts, while practising manifestation techniques for a cash windfall. This way you'll be doubling your chances of success and sending out a powerful message that you're financially savvy and ready to receive more.

Set Yourself Small Challenges

Manifestation only works when you really believe in what you are doing. If you expect the outcome then you're likely to receive it, but to do this you have to place a certain amount of trust in the universe and in your own ability to generate positive energy and make things happen. As your manifesting skills grow, so will your confidence, so while you might want to go full steam ahead and manifest big changes, it's important to start with something you know you can achieve.

Resist the urge to get carried away and manifest big things for your family and friends. This is about building self-belief and setting small, achievable goals. Think of it like starting work. On your first day you wouldn't expect be to chairing meetings and giving presentations; you'd keep it simple and stick with tasks that help you familiarize yourself with how the office works and your new colleagues. Manifesting works in the same way. You need to get to grips with the techniques and working with the universe before you can handle more ambitious requests.

YOUR MOTIVATION

For this first exercise, you'll need a sheet of paper and a pen.

- Ask yourself the question 'what do I want right now?', then list at least five things that come to mind.

- For each item on the list, ask 'why do I want this?', then write down the first thing that comes into your head.

- Take your time and look at what you've written. As you reflect on each one, you'll see motives emerge and you'll understand what drives your desires – this is what you really need to manifest.

- To finish, highlight key words that sum up your motivation for each item on the list.

CLOSER FAMILY TIES - INTENTIONS

For this challenge, you can practise developing your technique, adding each new skill as you acquire them. Let's say your intention is to achieve a closer connection with your friends and family. Perhaps you'd like to improve the way you communicate so that you understand each other at a deeper level.

• Think about your motives and what it is you really want to achieve. Make your intention clear.

• Think about manifesting a deeper connection between you. In this case, you might take a two-pronged approach, where you focus on the joy that you share when you're together with your friends and family, as well as improving the way you communicate.

• This practice in identifying your objectives will enable you to understand and apply the manifestation techniques you will learn in the following chapters.

• Put this to one side and revisit it as you learn each new technique.

Acknowledge Your Success

Every time you manifest something, acknowledge your success and build upon it. Take it step by step and mark the stages of your progress. Even if things don't work out as planned, you'll be able to see what works for you and what you can improve. This, in turn, builds self-belief in your skills.

Small victories count at every stage when you're manifesting, and it's important to acknowledge them in some way, whether you choose to share your success with those close to you, do something to celebrate the achievement, or write down what worked and why. When you recognize success in this way, you focus on the positives and this raises your energy vibration and helps you attract even more.

Mark Up Your Results

Think about creating a chart that you can pin on a notice board and mark up your progress, or give yourself a gold star each time you succeed. Look for inspiration online, or simply draw something on paper. The most important thing is that you recognize your success, even at these early stages, and mark it in some way. If you prefer, you could do this by treating yourself and celebrating the moment when you reach your goal.

Keep a Journal of Progress

It's helpful to keep a written record of your progress, and journaling is another important tool in the manifestation toolkit. You'll be able to reflect on the things you've tried that worked well, and the skills that might need developing. Giving yourself the space to evaluate your progress and express your thoughts opens up the channels of creativity so that ideas flow. You'll also find that organizing your thoughts in this way helps you identify new goals and the steps needed to make them happen.

JOURNALING

- Invest in a special notebook for your journaling, something that appeals to the eye and makes you want to open up the pages.

- Use the journal to chart every aspect of your manifestation journey. For now, you can set your intentions, organize your thoughts and write down any ideas as well as recording any successes that you have.

- Later on, you will begin to add details of the techniques you are employing to manifest your goal.

- Choose a set time every week to write in your journal. You might choose the end of the week so that you can reflect on what has happened, or the beginning of the week so that you can set targets.

- If you plan on doing lots of different types of manifestation you might want to invest in more than one journal, so you could have one for personal wishes and material items, and one that relates to study and career aspirations.

- If you're not a fan of handwriting, you can create a journal online in a similar way and document your progress using your laptop or phone. You might even want to share it with like-minded friends and ask for their advice and feedback.

Building Your Skills

Here are ten mini-manifestations so you can exercise the skills you have learnt in this chapter. Think about each one and write down a specific personal goal related to that subject. Think about your current situation in each area. Finally consider why it is important to you.

1. Manifest calm.

2. Manifest compassion.

3. Manifest a positive attitude.

4. Manifest strong relationships.

5. Manifest balance.

6. Manifest patience.

7. Manifest generosity.

8. Manifest hope.

9. Manifest self-control.

10. Manifest self-esteem.

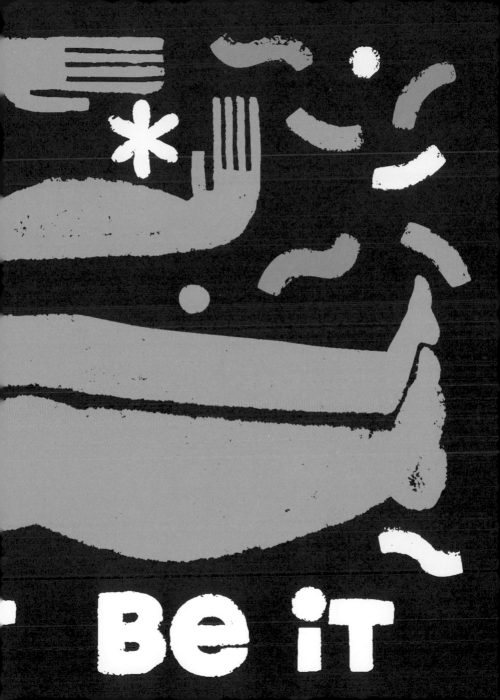

The Basics

A vision board is a visual representation of what you'd like to manifest in your life. It's a collage of hope and expectations that you build, using images, quotes, words and pictures that capture the essence of what you'd like to attract. A vision board can be created using a poster or white board that you display somewhere in your room, or you can build a digital version that you carry with you on your phone or laptop (see pages 44-45). The reason it works so well is that it draws on your experiences and what is important to you, so each picture, snippet or symbol resonates with you at a personal level. It helps to focus your thoughts to put you in the right mindset to attract goals – and it's also immediate in its effect, in that you look at it and instantly know what it represents. It reinforces the message you want to send to the universe in a clear, concise way. Making a vision board is also fun to do and allows you to unleash your creative side, which is an important part of the manifesting process.

You don't have to be particularly crafty to get to grips with a vision board. At the end of the day you are the only person who will see it (unless you choose to share it). It's more about defining your intention, collecting the pictures and quotations that represent your wishes, and displaying them in a way that expresses your request. Think of it like a dream board, and a way to focus your mind.

How It Works

Vision boards are a powerful, practical tool that anyone can use and they work in a number of ways. We know that what we focus on expands, and if we pour our attention into one thing, then we'll likely attract more of the same; this is a universal law (see page 19). A vision board helps you condense your dreams into one space. It gives you a focus that you can look at every day and it helps you visualize your aims. Concentrating on the things you want puts you in the right mindset to recognize and seize opportunities as they arise and work with the energy of abundance.

Of course, you have to put the work in too, not only in creating a board that sums up your wishes but also working with it every day. It's important to set aside time to look at your board and think about what it means to you. It also helps if you use other complementary manifesting tools such as visualizations and affirmations (see chapters five and seven) alongside the board, to boost your chances of success. You should be prepared to take positive action when the opportunity arises and take steps towards your goal. Working in unison with your board in all of these ways will help you get the results you want.

Different Types of Vision Board

Vision boards can be anything you want them to be, from collages on paper or board, to something more high-tech and digital, which allows you to pin items and words that appeal to you online. Whichever route you choose, you'll have to take the same approach and have a clear idea of what you want to manifest, but the first step is deciding which type of vision board is right for you.

Digital Boards

Going digital has lots of benefits. Whether you choose something like a Pinterest board or an online template, they're easy to work with and you don't have to spend time collecting pictures and snippets from magazines. You can 'pin' pictures that you come across to create the look you want and you'll be able to update your vision board easily and switch styles whenever you want. There are plenty of online platforms and tools that can help you. Once you've created your board, you'll be able to download it to all your devices, print it out, and even share it on social media, if you want to.

Collage Boards

A collage vision board that you create yourself takes some time and planning, but the amount of effort you put in is rewarded in kind. The time you spend planning and gathering the right kind of images and clippings helps to hone your focus and sends a very clear message to the universe. You'll also be engaging your imagination. This allows ideas to flow and puts you in the creative zone, which is exactly where you need to be to achieve any kind of goal. You are completely in control of the process and how the board looks, and it will be unique to you. Giving yourself this kind of creative power is a vote of confidence in your abilities to manifest, which boosts self-belief and affects the outcome in a positive way. It also allows you some screen-free time to enjoy being creative.

Still unsure which type of board is for you?

A practical collage vision board is the one for you if ....

- you like pouring through pictures and images in magazines

- you like to spend time thinking about the design of something, whether that's the way your bedroom looks or putting together an outfit to wear

- you enjoy the creative process, no matter how long it takes

A digital board is the one for you if ...

- you're constantly spotting images and ideas that you love on social media

- you're not worried about having a physical board, and you're happy to take a back seat with design, as long as you can control the content

- you find it easy to focus on pictures on your phone/laptop and immerse yourself in that world

Themes and Ideas

Whether you're looking to update your wardrobe and go for whole new look, or you want to create more peace and balance in your life, there's a way to do it using a vision board. You can have boards for mini goals and boards from much bigger lifelong projects. You can have boards that reflect your heart's desires and those that are geared towards more material things.

Once you've decided on your intention, it's about gathering together things that represent your goal and resonate with you. You might have images in mind, or favourite quotes that you can incorporate. The key here is to keep your eyes open for ideas and if you see anything that calls to you, find a way to use it. The board is personal to you, so it doesn't matter if it doesn't mean the same thing to someone else. As long as you recognize the deeper meaning, that's all that counts.

Consider the themes you are working with in your vision board. Suppose you'd like to meet someone special, then your themes might be fun, love and romance, so you'll be looking for pictures, words and cuttings that symbolize these things. You might go for popular symbols like hearts, cupids and roses, and you might also want to include pictures of couples together, quotes from love poems, or a picture of yourself taken when you felt truly loved. If you want to manifest a holiday with friends you might include postcards of places you'd like to visit, pictures of sandy beaches and photos of your besties. If you are after a new job, it might be a laptop or a smart office.

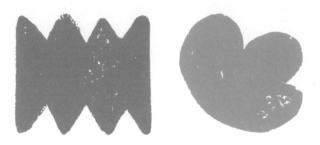

Planning Your Vision Board

Your vision board is as individual as you are. It's a way of expressing your wishes through images and key words, and also putting your unique stamp on it. After all, no-one knows you like yourself! Once you have a clear intention of what you want to manifest, spend some time reflecting on what this means to you.

Consider the layout of the board and how you might group items together. It's entirely up to you if you want to designate areas of your board to specific themes, or you want to be more general and just go with your creative flow. How you arrange the images and quotes is your personal choice and you'll instinctively know when a design feels right.

Make notes and let ideas, words and images come naturally, perhaps starting with a roughly-sketched plan, then adding specific drawings to create a collage effect.

If you prefer, you can gather the images you're going to use by scouring magazines and newspapers, books, personal photographs and online. This is about your interpretation of your wish, so if a picture captures your interest or reflects some part of it, then use it. Symbols can also be used to represent what you'd like to manifest. Remember, nothing is set in stone and you can change things at any time.

Be sure to engage your imagination and enjoy this part of the process. Daydream, doodle and have fun. Vision boards are a creative tool and a way of communicating who you are and what you want, so keep this in mind when coming up with ideas and collecting images.

Key words are also an important feature, so keep an eye out for phrases, poems or sentences that catch your attention and resonate with your intention.

Anything you can do to enhance the impact of your board will boost your chances of success, so consider how you can hone your message to make the most of this manifesting tool.

PICTURE YOUR POTENTIAL
RE YOUR POTENTIAL • PICTURE YOU
TIAL • PICTURE YOUR POTENTIAL
RE YOUR POTENTIAL • PICTURE YOU
TIAL • PICTURE YOUR POTENTIAL
RE YOUR POTENTIAL • PICTURE YOU
TIAL • PICTURE YOUR POTENTIAL
URE YOUR POTENTIAL • PICTURE YOU
NTIAL • PICTURE YOUR POTENTIAL
RE YOUR POTENTIAL • PICTURE YOU
TIAL • PICTURE YOUR POTENTIAL
URE YOUR POTENTIAL • PICTURE YOU
TIAL • PICTURE YOUR POTENTIAL
URE YOUR POTENTIAL • PICTURE YOU
TIAL • PICTURE YOUR POTENTIAL
URE YOUR POTENTIAL • PICTURE YOU
TIAL • PICTURE YOUR POTENTIAL
URE YOUR POTENTIAL • PICTURE YOU

FOCUS YOUR MIND

You will need a sheet of paper and a pen or your laptop or phone for this.

- Write down in a couple of sentences what you're hoping to manifest. Be as specific as you can, so you might say, 'I want to manifest my dream apartment, with beautiful furniture and views of the city'.

- Picture the apartment in your head and think of the first few words that come to mind. Write these words down.

- Give yourself a few minutes and focus on your breathing. Quieten your mind and relax.

- When you're ready, think of a few more words to describe the apartment. Be creative and challenge yourself to come up with something different – something you've never said before.

- When you've finished, look at both sets of words and pick out the most important ones. You'll find that you can take words from both sections and come up with something perfect that matches how you think and feel about your potential new home.

- The challenge works by comparing the two sets of words. The first set is your instinctual response and the second set allows you to be more reflective and creative and engage your imagination. Taking the best from both, you should have a fully rounded picture from which you can build your vision board and find the right images, words and phrases that will bring it to life.

- Make sure you place your board somewhere that you can see it every day, for example, above your desk, or by your bed so that you view it morning and night. If your board is digital, set an alarm on your phone to remind you to view it at set times during your day, or make it your screen saver.

- When you look at your board, imagine you already have your goal and how this will feel. Visualize the moment when you have what you want and connect with your emotions.

- When you're scrolling on your phone, keep an eye open for new things that you can add to your vision board.

- When you look at your board, take in every aspect and think about the images and words that you've used and why you chose them. Use the board as a creative trigger and let your mind wander so that other images and words associated with your dream flow into your head. Make a note of any that stand out and add them to your board.

- State your intention in the form of an affirmation that complements the theme of your board. For example, if you want to leave home and find your own place, you might say, 'I am independent and ready to make my way in the world.' Repeat this affirmation every time you look at your board.

CLOSER FAMILY TIES - VISION BOARD

Pick up the project where you left it (on page 34) and create a vision board that relates to your new, closer relationship with your friends or family.

- On your board, you might include pictures of you with your family and friends, mementos of special times shared together and images that make you feel happy.

- You might also include words that promote a sense of closeness like 'love' and 'connection'.

Ten Ideas for Your First Vision Board

Here are some ideas for topic areas on your vision boards to get you started.

1. For peace and balance
Images and objects that inspire you from the natural world: mountains, beaches, shells etc. Calming colours and quotes that soothe your mind.

2. For energy
Pictures that represent fitness and movement for you: sports, sunshine, cheering crowds. Energizing quotes and images of healthy foods.

3. For money
Money symbols, gold coins, blank cheques, amounts of money you'd like to attract. Photos of beautiful houses and lavish lifestyles.

4. For success in any area
Quotes that inspire confidence and success, images of winners reaching the finish line and audiences clapping. Photos of role models or celebrities who have inspired you.

5. For travel
Tickets, pictures of aeroplanes, trains, boats, images of places you'd like to go, quotes and snippets of different languages and cuisines.

The **MORE** energy you **GiVE**, the **MORE** you'll **ReCeiVe**

6. **For love**
Pictures of happy couples, love symbols like hearts and flowers, quotes and romantic poetry.

7. **For mental health**
Calming images and photos of seascapes and blue skies, quotes and affirmations that promote good mental health and make you feel at peace.

8. **For luck**
Lucky symbols like a four-leaf clover or a horseshoe, lucky numbers, your own personal lucky colours or images, pictures of celebrations, affirmations like 'I am lucky'.

9. **For happiness**
Photos of happy times with your friends or family, specific memories that make you smile, places that lift your spirits, uplifting quotes and affirmations.

10. **For creativity**
Images that make you feel creative, photos of the natural world, quotes from your favourite writers, pictures of books, films or songs that have inspired you.

Words and Stories

We are all storytellers. It's how we learned to make sense of the world and build a common landscape. It's also the way we connect and bond with others. Everyday conversation is made up of thousands of stories, but the ones we tell ourselves are by far the most powerful. The narratives that you play over in your mind create your reality, so if you want to change that reality you need to switch up the story

Scripting is one of the best ways to do this. It's an effective manifestation tool and ideal for those who prefer to work with words, or find they're not drawn to creating a vision board. It can also be used alongside any of the other techniques in this book to boost your chances of manifestation success. The idea is that you create a script which fits with what you want. It's like telling yourself a story, over and over again. The key is to imagine that you've already manifested your desire. You are living that life and experiencing the joy. Essentially you're daydreaming, but instead of just thinking things through, you'll actually be putting pen to paper, or typing out your unique story.

The good news is that scripting can be done anytime and anywhere. You can dig out your smartphone and make some notes while you're on your morning commute, keep a journal with you and add to it in your breaks or at lunch time at work or during study, or make a regular slot in your diary for scripting. All you need are a few basic tools, a bit of time and space and your imagination.

Eliminating Need

You can have different scripts for different things that you want to manifest, or you can be creative and come up with a number of scripts that all work towards the same goal. It's about jumping forward into the future that you want and making it the present. The reason this works is because it eliminates the 'need' you have, which creates the distance between you and what you want to manifest. When you want something, it is often out of reach. The more you want it, the more out of reach it can feel. When you have something, you no longer need it. You can see it, feel it, enjoy it, and this not only raises your energy vibration, it sends a powerful message to the universe to give you more of the same.

• Be THE auTHOR OF YOUR STORY •

Getting Started

To give you an idea of how a script works and the kind of thing you should be aiming for, let's imagine a scenario. You're ready to buy your first car; this is what you'd like to manifest. You know exactly what type of car you want and you have a clear intention in mind. Now jump forwards and imagine what it would be like to have that car; picture a day in your life and start your story at the beginning.

Sample Script

I am looking forward to the day ahead, to going on an adventure in my gorgeous red Volkswagen Beetle. I have the keys in my hand and it feels so good to know that this is mine and that I have the freedom to drive anywhere I want. I open my front door, and there it is, sitting outside my home. The red paintwork gleams in the morning sun. I press the key and hear the familiar trill as the door unlocks. My chariot awaits. I slide my hand beneath the handle and the door swings open. The interior is plush and smooth, dark but inviting, and the heady aroma of leather fills the air. I breathe in and enjoy the smell of newness. I slip onto the seat and sit back. It is the perfect fit. I feel safe and cushioned, ready to begin my adventure.

This is a starter script. You might choose to tell the story of taking a road trip, going out with friends, or whatever brings it alive for you. It's up to you which narrative you choose as long as it's in the present and you can immerse yourself in the script and believe that you are there.

Some Scripting Pointers

Here are some tips to help you get the most out of
your scripting.

Experience in the Present

Always keep the narrative in the present tense. Remember,
what you want is no longer out of reach; you have it and
you are experiencing it right now, so live in the moment.
Use words like 'I am' or 'I have' rather than 'I will be' or
'I will have'. It's easy to fall into the trap of putting what
you want in the future because in reality it's not yours yet,
so take your time and read through your script in stages
to make sure you are living the dream in the present.

Engage All Your Senses

Bring your script to life by making it as real as possible.
Engage all your senses and think about what you can
see, hear, smell, taste and feel. For example, you've got
your dream summer dress on and you're wearing it at
the poolside bar on holiday. How does it make you feel?
What is like to move in the dress? Perhaps you notice how
it feels against your skin or how the colour complements
your skin tone. You can smell the delicate scent of the
material combined with your favourite fragrance. It might
seem over the top when you're writing it but it will help
you make it a 3D experience. Imagine it's a film and you're
walking through it in your mind. Who else is there? How do
others see you? Include as much detail as you can to give
you the best chance of getting exactly what you want.

Think About How You Feel

Consider how you'll feel when you have manifested what you want. To help you do this, spend some time thinking about the emotions as well as the practicalities and put yourself in that place. Make a list of feelings and read through it so that you have a clear idea in your mind of what this will mean for you. As you script, remember to talk about your emotions, as this will help to add depth to your story and bring it to life, while also sending a powerful message to the universe.

Be Authentic

It can be hard to imagine what it's like to have something in your life if you've never experienced it before, so do your research. If you're looking for a specific job, get to know as much as you can about it. Talk to those already in the position and get an idea of what an average day might involve. Seek common ground and recall moments in your life when you might have achieved something similar. For example, if you want to ace an interview, you might think back to a previous situation where you've faced a panel or had to give a presentation and you impressed. Draw on those experiences to build your manifesting script.

Look at Your Script From Different Perspectives

Broaden your horizons and think of scenarios that you can use as different scripts to manifest the same thing. For example, you'd like to manifest a romantic partner, so you might start with a script that describes your first meeting, how your eyes met across the room, what you said or what you felt. This is a great start, but don't just focus on that one moment in your life together. Move on and describe your first date, or the moment you realized that you were soulmates, happy times shared together, your first meal out, trip away and so on. Experiment and have fun with the scripting process. When you let your imagination have free rein, you naturally put more positive energy and belief into manifesting what you want.

Using Storyboards

Storyboards work in a similar way to a script, but they use less text and a combination of words, images and symbols to tell the story and help you manifest your goals. They can be a simple three-box narrative with a beginning, a middle and an end, or more detailed narrative with any number of boxes to mark the stages. You don't have to be good at drawing to make them work. If you prefer to use bullet points within each box rather than images to tell the tale, that's fine. Think of the layout like a comic book, with a series of boxes with pictures that tell the story, along with captions to describe what's happening. Sometimes you might have dialogue between the characters.

To start, you need to think about what you want and identify your intention. Then imagine you're telling the story of how you got there using a combination of pictures and key sentences.

STORYBOARD

Imagine you want to secure a place at the university or college of your choice; this is what you'd like to manifest. Remember, you can choose the simplest of images – you don't have to be an Andy Warhol.

- Take a sheet of paper, turn it lengthways and draw three large boxes next to each other.

- The first box is the beginning of your story, so this is where you identify the university or college, and the grades you need to get there. You might want to write a series of bullet points describing this or draw a picture of the university sign with the name clearly on display and then write a sentence beneath.

- The second box sees you putting in the work: revising, researching, and then finally taking your exam and feeling you've done your best. Again, find a way to tell this part of the tale using pictures, sentences or bullet points, so you might have an image of a book to represent you revising, or a sketch of a sheet of paper with exam written at the top.

- The third and final box sees you achieving the grades you need and celebrating when you receive your offer letter, so you might want to simply highlight the grades that you want in this box.

- Look at the storyboard you have created and run through it in your mind several times. How does it make you feel?

- Think of one word to sum up that feeling, so you might choose 'elated' or 'excited'.

- Write the word down somewhere on the storyboard and think of an affirmation to go with it, something like 'I am excited that I am going to ... university'.

- Every day, read through your storyboard, take in the images and repeat your affirmation.

CLOSER FAMILY TIES – SCRIPTING AND STORYBOARDS

Now go back to your step-by-step project (see page 53) and strengthen your manifestation by trying one – or more – of the visualization techniques in this chapter.

- Write out a story about your success, keeping it positive and adding plenty of detail. Remember to include how you feel.

- Talk about how friends or other family members react to you.

- You may prefer to do a storyboard – a comic strip presentation of where you want to be in relation to your friends and family.

- Writing a script or narrative is a key part of manifesting, but to keep the energy fresh and moving forwards it's important to make it a part of your routine. Add extra material as and when you can; tweak, rewrite and create new scripts when you feel inspired.

- Make a point of reading and repeating the narrative as often as you can throughout the day. To help, have regular time slots, such as first thing in morning before breakfast and last thing at night before bed.

- It's not always possible to read your script out loud, depending on where you are, but when you do have a quiet moment to yourself make a point of doing this. Put all your emotions into it and imagine you're giving a performance.

- Working with narratives – whether you're scripting or putting together a story – is a fun thing to do. It taps into your innate creativity and helps to flex your imagination. Enjoy the process and trust in your ability to create the future you desire.

Ten Ideas for Your First Script or Narrative

If you need some suggestions for trying out narratives, experiment with these ideas.

1. Making new friends

Describe meeting a new group of friends and enjoying their company, laughing together and connecting. Perhaps they invite you to go shopping with them, or to hang out somewhere? Describe each scenario separately.

2. Acing an interview

Describe the interview setting and see yourself answering the questions with confidence. What was it like to notice the positive reaction of the panel? Take this further and describe the moment when you hear you are successful.

3. Your first day at university

Describe how excited you feel as you enter the building for the first time. Then talk about how you feel at the end of the day and how much you enjoyed the experience.

4. Your first day at work

Describe how welcome everyone made you feel and how you settled in. Remember to engage your emotions and describe how you'd like to feel in your new job. See yourself in the role a month from now, and describe getting ready for work and looking forward to the day ahead.

5. Your first date

Describe meeting your date in person, where you go and what you do. Describe how you feel at the time, the anticipation and excitement. Think of the conversations you might have and how you might plan your next date.

6. Impressing in a presentation

Describe the room, the people, how you feel and then the moment when you take the floor. Describe how you'll deal with questions effectively and engage with your audience. Finally talk about the positive reaction you get and how confident this makes you feel.

7. Winning at something

Focus on describing the moment when you win and do this in detail. How do you feel? What have you won? Where are you and what do you do? What are you going to do next? Bring those joyful emotions to life in your description.

8. Moving into your own place

Imagine unlocking the door for the first time and entering your new apartment. Walk through each room and describe it in detail. How does it make you feel to know that this is your new home?

9. Moving in with friends or your partner

Describe waking up in your new home with your flatmates or your partner. How do you feel? What is the moment like when you wake up and become aware that you have started this new life? Describe the place in detail.

10. Meeting your partner's parents

Describe the scenario when you meet your partner's parents, whether this is in their home or somewhere like a coffee shop or a restaurant. Imagine yourself feeling comfortable and confident during the meeting. Look into the future and see yourself sharing a family meal with them, feeling relaxed and happy in their company.

Tool and tricks

Manifesting is a powerful tool, and there are many things you can do to enhance your chances of getting results. Simple shifts in your attitude and small changes in the way you think and talk to yourself make a huge difference. From making statements, known as affirmations, to the universe about your life and what you want, to giving thanks for all the blessings you already have, you can not only turn things around but also make life more enjoyable. Manifesting shouldn't be a struggle; it is a positive and pro-active experience that can benefit you in many ways.

Affirmations and How to Use Them

Imagine you're preparing for a big night out. You're looking forward to it, you've put in the work and planned everything from when you'll meet up with your friends to booking your taxi home, now all you have to do is wait – and that's the exciting part. During the lead up, you will probably discuss your plans with friends and family, you'll talk excitedly about how amazing it will be, and these statements will increase the pleasure and fulfilment you feel when the big night finally arrives.

Affirmations work in a similar way. They are positive statements that you can repeat throughout the day – both in your head and out loud – to reinforce your request to the universe. They can be used alongside other manifesting techniques, such as narratives or scripting, and they can also be added to your vision board so that every time you see it, you repeat the affirmation and reaffirm your intent. Affirmations put you in the right mindset and help you to think and act positively until you achieve your goal. They also serve as a reminder to the universe, like saying, 'I'm here and I'm ready for ... to come into my life.'

There are three main rules when working with affirmations.

Stay in the Present
Always word your statement in the present, for example 'I am going to attract the perfect partner,' becomes 'I attract the perfect partner.' When we say 'I am going to' we place what we want in the future, putting it further away from us. When we say 'I attract, or I am attracting' we are making it happen, right now, which brings our desire even closer.

Use Positive Vocabulary
Choose positive words instead of negative, so if you want to get healthy and lose a few pounds it's better to say, 'I am making healthy food choices', rather than 'I do not eat junk food any more.' Negative words act in a negative way and negate the power of the affirmation. Positive words encourage us to take action, and create positive energy, which is exactly what you need, because like attracts like.

Fake It Till You Make It
Affirmations are most effective when repeated out loud, but it's important to say it like you mean it, even if you don't. Make your affirmations count by thinking about each word and if you don't really feel it, fake it till you make it! Repeat the affirmation over and over and pretend until your heart and mind catch up. Not only will you feel better and brighter, but you'll also power up your manifesting at the same time.

Getting the Most Out of Affirmations

Affirmations are so important that it is worth going over the main points of how to maximize their effectiveness.

- Repetition is key with affirmations: the more you say something and believe it, the more likely the universe will hear and give you what you want, so make a point of repeating your affirmation throughout the day. Slot some affirmation spots into your diary, like any other practice, at regular intervals.

- Take the time out to meditate on your affirmation. Sit with the words in your mind and focus on the deeper meaning. See the affirmation manifest in your mind and imagine what that would feel like.

- Note down your affirmations and pin them up where you will see them every day. You could stick them around your mirror, on the fridge or keep them in your purse.

- Create a screensaver using your affirmation. Use bright, engaging graphics and set it on your phone/tablet/laptop, so that you'll see it every time you open them.

- Write an email to yourself that includes your affirmation in the title. In the body of the email describe what it feels like to have what you want in your life. Send the email to yourself and make a point of re-reading it when you need to.

The Power of Gratitude

Gratitude is one of the most powerful manifesting tools. When you give thanks for something, it's like shining a light on all the good stuff, and saying to the universe: 'thank you, and please send more!'. It puts you in the flow of abundance and also raises your vibrational energy. You switch up your mindset, which in turn makes you attuned to a higher frequency so that you attract positive energy into your life. It's also addictive. As you start to notice all the good stuff, your awareness expands and your general mood improves. You'll feel less stressed and more able to deal with any setbacks and blocks during your manifestation journey.

Once you get into the habit of giving thanks, you'll find you naturally focus on all the great things in your life instead of looking for the bad. Instead of focusing on what you don't have, you'll recognize the blessings that the universe has already given you and attract even more.

make 'THANK YOU' YOUR NEW MANTRA

Gratitude Journal
To help you adopt an attitude of gratitude, try this:

If you have already started journaling, well done! If not, now's the time to start. Get yourself a notebook and use it to note down the things you're grateful for. Make a point of writing five things at the end of every day that you're thankful for, then over time increase the number to ten. Be specific and pick out details and special moments, like being grateful for a pep talk from your best friend that lifted your spirits. At the end of each week, re-read all the entries and remind yourself of all the wonderful blessings in your life. Dip into the journal every time you need a pick-me-up, to boost positive energy.

Say 'Thank You'
Make 'thank you' your new mantra and say it often. Think of all the people you encounter in your day who deserve a 'thank you', whether that's for something they do now or have done in the past. Be bold and say 'thank you' and 'I appreciate you' as often as you can, and don't be afraid to use it with strangers.

Say 'thank you' to yourself, too. Thank your body for keeping you active and mobile and your mind for coming up with brilliant ideas.

Finally say 'thank you' to the universe for the flow of abundance in your life.

Acknowledge Your Successes

It's important to recognize all the things you do well, and to give thanks for small victories. Sing your own praises and say, 'I deserve this, I smashed it!' Then do something to mark the occasion, whether that's a solo celebration, a treat for achieving your goal, or something bigger that you do with friends and family. Recognize your strengths and talents and be grateful for those moments when you attain success. When you do this, you instantly raise your energy vibration and send a powerful message to the universe that you're a winner.

Create a Blessings Box

Invest in a keepsake box that you can fill with things that will remind you of all the blessings in your life. You can use it to show your gratitude for the people, places and things that make your life special. Include pictures, quotes, notes and mementos that take you to your 'happy place' and remember to keep adding items, as this will keep the energy fresh and moving in the right direction. You can also do this digitally, by creating a folder on your phone or laptop, then make a point of keeping an eye out for things that you can put in your blessings file.

- Stand in front of a mirror every morning.

- Look yourself confidently in the eye, smile and say your affirmation out loud, three times.

- Each time you say it, think about every single word and what it means.

- Embrace your power and believe you have the ability to manifest whatever you need, right now.

CLOSER FAMILY TIES - AFFIRMATIONS

Complete your step-by-step project (see page 72) by writing some affirmations, following the advice in this chapter.

- See if you can come up with three or four really strong affirmations that you can repeat as often as you like.

- By practising all of the techniques you might find that your relationships improve on all levels. You form a tighter bond with your friends and can open up about the things that bother you, and you find yourself having more fun with family members.

AFFIRMATION PLUS GRATITUDE EQUALS POWER

Combine the power of affirmations with the positivity of gratitude.

- When you get up in the morning, think of one thing you're grateful for - so you might choose to be thankful for the new day ahead, or for your healthy body, which propels you forward.

- Now have a go at creating an affirmation for this, so you might say, 'I give thanks for this exciting new day and all the wonderful things it holds.'

- Write this down and keep it with you so that you can read and repeat it at intervals throughout your day.

- When something good happens, bring your attention back to the affirmation and repeat it once more.

- In the evening, before bed, run through the day and find five things that you are grateful for. Re-live any special moments in your mind.

- To finish, repeat your affirmation one more time.

make a
state-
ment

Ten Affirmations to Help You Manifest Anything

Remember to repeat your chosen affirmations as often as you can.

1. 'I am ready to live the life of my dreams.'

2. 'I trust in the power of the universe.'

3. 'I embrace and shape my destiny.'

4. 'Everything is working out perfectly for me right now.'

5. 'Manifestation is my superpower.'

6. 'The universe supports me in all I do.'

7. 'I am worthy of all I desire.'

8. 'Everything I want is mine.'

9. 'I expect, I believe, I receive.'

10. 'I am the author of my own life.'

Blocks to Manifesting

To make your manifesting a success, you need to be aware of the obstacles that might block your path. These are the things that will delay the attainment of your goals and can prevent them from happening at all. The good news is, once you know what kind of obstacle you're dealing with, you also know how to overcome it. With practice and effort, you'll be able to perfect your manifesting technique and make it even more effective. It doesn't matter if your goal is something small, like manifesting that outfit you've had your eye on for ages, or a bigger life goal like living in your own place or smashing your first job interview, the obstacles are always there. Knowing how to handle them puts you ahead of the game.

Limiting Beliefs

One of the biggest blocks to manifestation is holding on to limiting beliefs. These are the deep-seated ideas and behaviours that you have learnt over the years, so they're ingrained into your way of thinking. Often these beliefs come from your family and are passed down the generations. From ideas that at first seem simple and based on popular sayings like 'money doesn't grow on trees' to beliefs that have formed in response to your experiences; for example you may believe that there is only one soul mate for you, and because of this, you limit yourself from meeting any number of people who would be a good match. Limiting beliefs might not surface at first or seem important when you start manifesting, but they will hinder your progress. For example, if you want to manifest a cash windfall but you've always believed that it is a struggle to make money, then this belief will manifest and you'll find it hard to attract the cash.

How to Combat Limiting Beliefs

The best way to combat limiting beliefs is to address each one and ask yourself why you feel that way. What has created this belief? Is it based on the truth or is it just something that you've accepted without really thinking about it? Challenge yourself to think in a more positive way, one that resonates with what you'd like to manifest. You can do this by thinking of real life examples and ask yourself if this has been true for you. Also focus on any successes that you have had.

Impatience

Manifesting is as much about patience as it is perseverance. There's a balance between the two, and a waiting period. You can use the most powerful manifestation tool but it doesn't mean you'll receive your goal any quicker. The universe has a time frame, so while you can put your plan in motion, it could take days, weeks or even months to come to fruition. During this time, impatience is likely to set in and you may start to feel frustrated. You may even doubt your manifesting skills, and this could cause a block to you getting what you want. It's important to remember that your thoughts shape your reality, so if you start to believe that it won't happen, then it's likely it won't.

Try Constant Reinforcement

You need to constantly reinforce the idea that you will achieve success, using positive thoughts, affirmations and visualizations. Also be aware that you need to be open to the flow of abundance from the universe, which means actively looking for opportunities and steps that you can

CLOSER FAMILY TIES – OBSTACLES

If you find that your step-by-step project (see page 87) is going nowhere, you might feel frustrated that nothing is happening which, in turn, creates a block to your success.

- Go back to the drawing board and think of a different way to manifest what you want and eliminate the obstacles to your success.

- Look through this chapter and identify your particular problem, then find imaginative ways to break down the barriers.

take to bring you closer to your goal. To help combat impatience, make a list of the techniques you can use to feel more positive and employ at least one every day.

Trying Too Hard

This might sound similar to impatience, but it's about being too pushy, charging forward with your manifestation and focusing solely on that. When you do this, you ignore other things like signs from the universe and genuine opportunities that will help you step closer to your desire. You are also less likely to be grateful for what you already have, which creates a sense of lack in your life. The result is that you are likely to create more of the same and never be truly happy with anything you do receive. The irony is that when we behave in this way, we create resistance. We push and push against the flow of abundance from the universe.

Show More Appreciation

Take a step back and be sure to appreciate what you already have. Make a list of the things you are grateful for, the everyday blessings that light up your world. Be sure to make this a regular practice, by finding at least five things at the end of each day that you are thankful for; this should help you relax and enjoy the present moment.

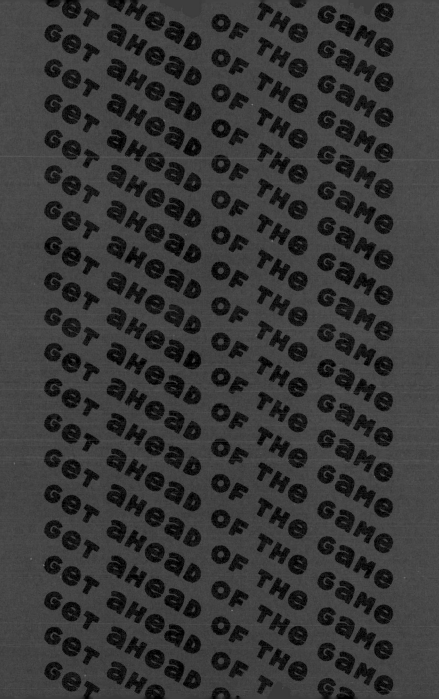

Fear of Loss

We can believe we want to manifest something, but we might not be fully ready for it, so we develop a fear of losing it before it's even ours. This fear of loss can be a huge obstacle to manifesting. Already we've switched our focus onto something negative which, in turn, creates worry and fear. The universe responds by withholding the one thing we really want, because we're not ready for it. Remember this is a collaboration, and you are meant to be working together in a positive way to achieve your dreams. Fear of loss also comes from a place of doubt. You doubt yourself and believe you don't deserve the thing that you really want to manifest – so much so, that you think you'll eventually lose it.

Work on Your Self-belief

The way to combat this obstacle is to work on your self-belief. Recognize your worth and know that you do deserve everything the universe can give you. Spend some time working on self-love, from valuing who you are as a person to treating yourself with care and kindness. Repeat positive affirmations and give thanks for all the wonderful things you already have in your life. These things are yours because you deserve them.

Focusing on What You Don't Want

When you place your attention on something, you direct your energy towards it and the universe responds by sending more of the same. Manifesting is about focusing on what you want, but often when we do this, we also find ourselves focusing on what we don't want. The two concepts go hand in hand. For example, you want to ace the job interview and so you imagine all of the ways it could go wrong, from saying the wrong thing to not saying anything at all. Even though these are things you don't want, you've switched your focus towards them. This is understandable but it also creates a huge obstacle when it comes to manifesting your desires.

Concentrate on Your Intention

Check in with yourself objectively on a regular basis and pay attention to your thoughts. If you find them shifting focus in this way, bring your attention back to the here and now and the idea that you already have what you want. Engage your emotions and imagine how you'll feel when you've manifested your desire.

Being Judgemental

This obstacle is about judging yourself and others, making comparisons and letting jealousy and envy be your main motivations for manifesting. It's natural that we might compare our lives to other people's and want what they have, but when it is at the forefront of your mind it lowers your energy vibration. Like any type of negativity, it also separates you from the flow of abundance from the universe. Even when the judgement is on yourself, it's easy to get caught up in negative emotions. You might be hard on yourself when you feel your manifestation isn't working as it should, which can also create a block.

Breathe

When you feel judgemental thoughts creeping into your mind, bring your attention back to your breathing. Draw a long deep breath in and count for four beats, then exhale and do the same. Focus on the rise and fall of your chest and let the thoughts float through your mind, rather than fixating on them.

Needing to Control the Outcome

To manifest successfully, you need to be able to define exactly what you want, adopt an attitude of self-belief and take positive action while at the same time relinquishing ultimate control. This last element can often be the hardest. When we know what we want, we assume that we also know how it will come to us. We have the end result in mind and may see it in a certain way, but the universe often has other ideas. It's important not to limit your manifesting by thinking your goals can only be achieved in one way.

Look Out for Unexpected Opportunities

Sometimes the exact thing we want comes to us in a very different package than we'd imagined. For example, you might want to boost your savings and think the best way to do this is to receive a cash windfall or a win. Instead, you find the money comes through an opportunity of some extra work outside your usual routine. The lesson here is not to worry about the how or why but to be open, let things happen and grab the opportunities as they arise. Let the process surprise you by saying to the universe, 'everything is happening exactly as it should'.

Stay Positive

Now you're aware of the some of the obstacles you may face, you can identify the ones that are likely to cause you the most problems. Address each one, and work on ways to overcome it. Sometimes the obstacle to your success is more general; perhaps you find it hard to maintain a positive outlook and need help eliminating negative thoughts and criticisms.

Silence Your Inner Critic

Your inner critic is the negative voice inside your head that surfaces and tries to create doubt and fear. It's the voice that tells you you're not good enough, not worthy, or that you can't do something even before you've tried. We all have this voice but for some it's more debilitating. If you want to become a manifesting genius it's important to gain control of the voice, learn how to stop it in its tracks and ultimately override it.

SILENCE YOUR INNER CRITIC

Practise breaking down the obstacles you encounter to ensure your success.

- When negative thoughts arise, recognize them for what they are and acknowledge that they are your inner critic trying to sabotage your happiness.

- Then shout 'stop!' as loudly as you can – whether that is actually out loud or in your head.

- Take a long deep breath in and, as you exhale, release any stress.

- Now think of a positive statement that you can make that replaces the negative words of your critic. For example, if you heard 'I can't do this, I'm useless at tests', replace it with 'I always give it my best. I can do this. I can ace this test'.

- Take a moment to breathe and repeat the positive statement in your mind.

Ten Practical Ways to Combat Negativity

Try these ideas or make a note of what you find fills you with positivity, then just do it!

1. Go outside for a walk and engage with your surroundings.

2. Do some exercise.

3. Connect with a friend – face to face, online or over a video call.

4. Listen to music or a podcast.

5. Cook your favourite meal.

6. Meditate.

7. Pamper yourself.

8. Immerse yourself in a book or magazine.

9. Chill out with a TV show you love.

10. Play your favourite song and sing along loudly.

Building Your Manifestation Toolkit

Manifestation comes in all shapes and forms and there are other techniques that you can use to create your reality. Some of these are best used in conjunction with vision boards and scripting, while others can be used as an alternative; some techniques can even be adapted to suit your specific needs. Once you have an understanding of how they work and a grasp of what to do, you can be flexible and create a manifesting toolkit that suits you.

Visualization

Visualization is a technique that you can use to manifest anything, and the good news is you can do it anytime and anywhere.

Visualization is mental rehearsal of reality. It allows you to experience what it is like to have what you want and walk through the process in your mind. Imagine having a cinema screen in your head and watching the film of your life unfold. You are the director, which means you can take the story anywhere. You have full control and you can put yourself in any situation you choose. In effect, visualization is a type of daydream but with a specific intention in mind. It's particularly effective if you're the kind of person who thinks visually and can focus on images, but even if you struggle, it's worth persevering. Even short, simple visualizations can help you attract the things you want, especially when combined with other tools like affirmations and positive thinking.

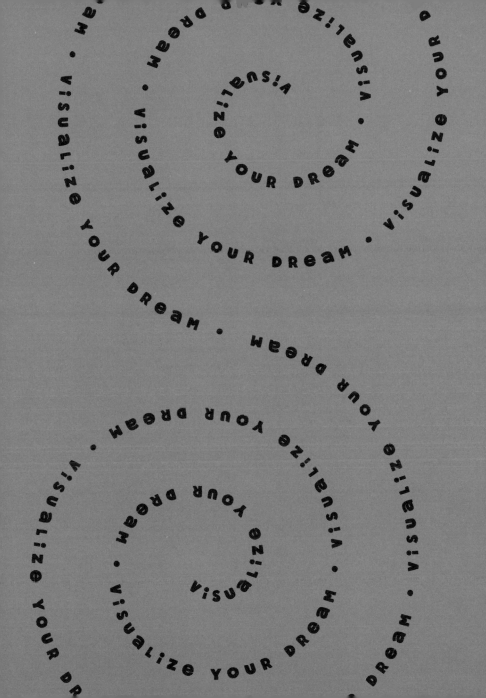

Picture the Day Ahead

Get into the habit of creating a mini visualization for your day ahead.

Take a few deep breaths to clear your head, then close your eyes. Picture a cinema screen behind your eyes. Slowly let your focus relax and let the film of your day unfold. Take it in stages, from your morning routine, moving through what you have planned for the rest of the day. See yourself completing any tasks successfully and catching up with friends and family. If you have anything specific that you'd like to achieve during your day, see yourself doing this in your mind. To finish, see yourself at the end of the day feeling happy and relaxed. Engage your senses and emotions and connect with your feelings. Run through it a few times.

Practising this exercise will help to strengthen your visualization skills and also act as a mini manifestation technique. At the end of the day you might want to check in with your original visualization and then consider how your day really went. Even if it didn't pan out exactly as you'd pictured it, you might see elements that came true from the things you experienced and how you felt emotionally.

See Your Life as You'd Like It To Be

Visualize your life as you'd like it to be and give yourself
a timeframe. Start off modestly, for example you might
want to visualize your life in a week's time. Think about
what you'd like to manifest during this time, write it down
and have a clear picture in your mind, then have a go at
seeing it in your mind. Bring it into the present. Once
you've successfully managed to run through this, give
yourself a bigger challenge. Visualize your life in a month's
time, and then a couple of months. Take your time and
enjoy the process of manifesting using the visual power of
your mind. This type of visualization is particularly effective
when you have a specific goal in mind, such as an exam or
a job interview.

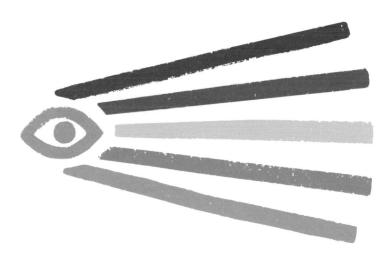

Visualization comes in many forms, and while it lends itself to telling a story, in part or fully, it can also be used to raise your vibration and attract positive energy.

The more you practise, the more proficient you will become at seeing yourself as you want to be.

visualization

- Close your eyes and spend a few minutes breathing deeply to clear your mind, then picture an enormous golden chute coming down from the sky above your head.

- The chute connects you to the powerful energy of abundance flowing from the universe.

- Picture a ray of golden light bursting from the chute and bathing you from head to toe in positive energy.

- Breathe it in. Absorb it. Let it seep under your skin.

- Continue to visualize this energy pouring down and showering you with blessings.

Meditation

Meditation is a powerful technique that opens your mind and brings you into alignment with the flow of abundance from the universe. It also raises your energy vibration and helps improve your focus and clarity, which is important for effective manifesting. Meditation heightens your awareness, meaning you're more likely to take inspired action towards your goal because it allows you to pick up on intuitive signs and messages from the universe.

Think of meditation as a type of mind training to prepare you for further manifestation work. It helps you become more self-aware and in touch with your needs, which helps you to identify goals. Used alongside visualization and positive thinking, it can help you create your future and attract positive energy. It's also a great way to flex your intuition and bring you into alignment with the universe.

Meditation can help you ignite your creative spark and encourage the flow of ideas for your manifesting. By clearing your mind and being fully present in the moment, you have the space and freedom to unleash your imagination.

Finally, meditation can help you break the spiral of negative thoughts if you find them trying to break your positivity.

BREATHE IN THE LIGHT

Raise your energy vibration to attract what you want by breathing in coloured light.

- Start by asking yourself which colour you associate with vibrant energy. You might want to close your eyes and ask this question, then see which colour springs to mind, or look at a selection of colours and see which one makes you feel happy and energized.

- Next close your eyes and focus on your breathing. Draw a long deep breath in and as you exhale, imagine releasing any negative thoughts or limiting beliefs that might hinder manifestation.

- Continue to breathe in a slow, steady loop, then when you are ready, focus on the colour of your choice.

- Imagine that as you inhale, you're drawing in this colour, taking it down into your chest and lungs. As you exhale, you're releasing negative energy.

- Continue to breathe in this way for five minutes. If your mind wanders, don't worry, simply bring it back to your breath and focus on the colour you have chosen.

How to Meditate

There are lots of meditation techniques, but this is a simple starting point. Take five to ten minutes every day and this will relax and clear your head. You'll restore focus and put yourself in a positive frame of mind.

- Sit or lie comfortably and relax your body as much as you can, especially your shoulders, where we often hold tension.

- Lengthen your spine and draw a deep breath in, then exhale to the count of four long beats.

- Focus on one thing that you can see and let your gaze soften. Notice everything you can about this object: take in its shape and form, size and structure. When you mind starts to wander, bring your attention back to this object and breathe.

- Take your time, slow your breathing right down and simply engage with the moment.

- Imagine drawing a stream of air up through the soles of your feet, along the length of your spine, over your head and out through your mouth as you exhale.

- Repeat this continual loop and focus on the journey of your breath. Let thoughts come and go but always bring your attention back to the breath.

- By time you've finished you should feel brighter, energized and inspired to manifest.

Positive Thinking

When you think positively, you are optimistic about the future. You adopt a constructive attitude that colours everything you do. Because your mind is open to possibilities, you can look for the best outcome to any situation, and you'll spot opportunities as they present themselves. This kind of outlook helps to raise your energy vibration, which ensures you send the right message to the universe. It's not always easy to remain positive, particularly when life throws you a curve ball, but there are things you can do to help change your attitude for the better and improve your chances of manifesting what you want.

Positive thinking complements any type of manifestation technique. It's something you should use alongside other practices to create your reality. Here are some of the ways that you can use positive thinking to help with manifestation.

Reframe Your Situation
When something unexpected or bad happens, try to reframe your thinking. Instead of focusing on the negative aspects, try and identify at least one positive aspect of the situation. For example, you might miss the bus and, yes, it's frustrating, but it gives you more time to listen to music, appreciate your surroundings, chat with other commuters or even get some exercise and walk instead. Getting into the habit of finding the positive spin on what is happening is particularly effective in manifestation as it means your mind is open to possibilities that you might otherwise miss. Plus it generates positive energy.

Picture Your Best Future

Daydream a little and imagine your future. Think about every aspect of your life, from your personal and home life to your career, leisure time, friends and hobbies. What would your ideal life look like? Create the best possible future in your mind and then write down what you see. Research suggests that when we focus on a bright future we create a positive outlook, feel happier and we can achieve more in the present, which is exactly what we need to do when manifesting. Positive thinking raises our energy vibration to new heights.

Smile and Focus

Smiling promotes positivity. It's one of the best ways to raise your energy vibration and to switch up your mindset. Smile and feel the expression light up your face. Smile at someone else and watch as they return the favour. Feel the positive energy flow between you. Smile and focus on a positive thought, even if it's something as simple as 'I am filled with positive energy, I manifest whatever I need'.

Know Your True Value

Positive thinking is never more important than when you're thinking about yourself and what you can do. To manifest effectively you have to believe that you are worthy and deserve to be happy. It makes sense, then, to celebrate all the good things that make you, you!

KNOW YOUR VALUE

- Make a list of your strengths and talents.

- If you're struggling to think of anything positive to say about yourself, ask friends and family to help. They will be able to highlight all the wonderful qualities that make you special.

- Once the list is complete, read it through and give thanks for everything you've noted.

- When you recognize your worth, you'll also see what you can achieve and that anything is possible.

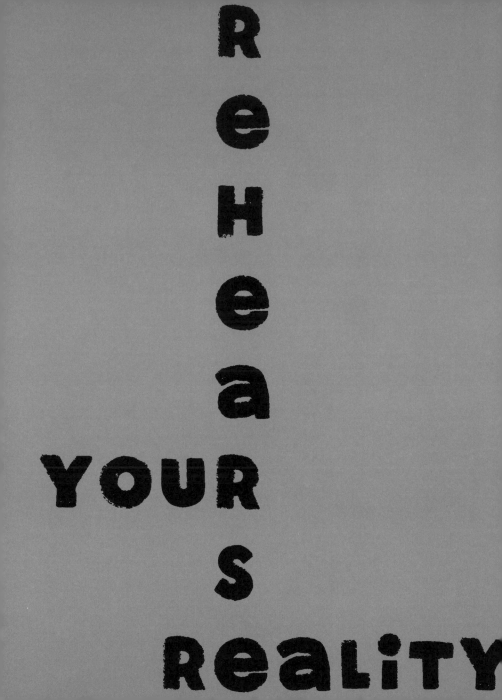

ReHeaRs

YOUR

ReaLiTY

Ten Ways to Boost Positive Thinking

Positive thinking is key to staying in the present and appreciating what you have and what you can achieve.

1. Tell yourself that it's going to be a great day.

2. Listen to an upbeat song.

3. Pay someone a compliment.

4. Say thank you for the good things in your life.

5. Give yourself permission to laugh, and laugh often.

6. Spend time with people who make you feel good.

7. Celebrate your successes.

8. Talk to yourself as you would talk to your best friend.

9. Relive positive moments by sharing them with others.

10. Do something kind for a complete stranger.

Manifesting for Others

Once you've got the hang of manifesting and honed your skills, you can try creating on a much wider scale. From bigger items and ideas to spreading the love and sharing your skills with friends, family and the community, the sky really is the limit when it comes to shaping your future. As long as you have a clear intention in mind and you can support this with other techniques, you can use your manifesting skills to help others, lead a more holistic lifestyle and to generate positive energy in any area.

Share the joy of manifesting with friends and family. Even if they're not on board with the process, you can help them attract the things they want with a few simple tips and tricks that you can incorporate into your own practice.

Visualizations

Visualizations are usually aimed at something you want, and the idea is you bring it into the present and imagine that you already have it. You can use the same process to make dreams come true for those closest to you.

Let's imagine that your mum wants to move house, but she's struggling to find the right place, in the right area for a price she can afford. Once you have a clear idea of exactly what it is your mum is looking for, then you can start the visualization process, so in this case you might visualize your mum waking up in her new home. You might see her in each room, enjoying the reality of her dream home. You might bring yourself into the visualization by visiting your mum in her new place and experiencing her new home for yourself, or perhaps you're already there sharing this new space with her. As you visualize, consider how it feels for both of you. Engage your senses and bring the place to life, then finish by making a clear statement to the universe, something like, 'As I see, let it be'.

Affirmations

Affirmations are statements that focus the mind and support other forms of manifestation. They can be tweaked to work on a much larger scale, and they're easy to use. Create affirmations that work for everyone, by making them universal, so if you want to manifest happiness you might say, 'I manifest a happy life for myself and my (friend/partner/dad/sister)' or 'Happiness fills the life of all those dear to me'.

When you say the affirmation, really think about your intention and what it would look like, for example, see your bestie looking happy and enjoying life.

Vision Boards

Vision boards are personal to you and should be filled with things that are associated with your desire, but you can make them all-encompassing by bringing in friends, family and the wider community. For example, if you're looking to find peace and balance and you want to bring that into your family life, you might incorporate images of family gatherings and affirmations that include your nearest and dearest. If you want to spread the love further to your community, you might include pictures that incorporate the surrounding area, important places in your local neighbourhood and people who make a difference.

Vision boards can work well when you focus on them in pairs, so if you've a willing friend, or a partner who wants to help, you can work on one together. The important thing is to identify your intention together and make it something that is important to you both.

CReaTe a ViSiON BOaRD WiTH YOUR PaRTNeR

Let's imagine that you're going to work on a vision board with your partner. You might be looking for your first home together, so your intention would be to find an apartment in your price range that you both love.

- Start by brainstorming ideas. Make a list of all the things that you want from this place. Daydream and come up with a vision that you both agree upon.

- Next give yourselves a minute to write down words that you might associate with the place, for example you might pick 'cosy', 'modern' and 'city living'.

- Compare notes on the words you have chosen and pick a selection that you can use on your board.

- Have fun sourcing images and quotes that capture the way you both feel about your new pad, then get creative and arrange them on your board.

- When you're happy with the picture you've created, come up with an affirmation that you can both use every day, as part of your manifesting ritual.

- To finish take pictures of the board so that you both have digital access, then agree on a set time every week when you will look at the vision board (even when you're apart) and repeat the affirmation.

Employ the Gratitude Attitude

If you want to move your manifesting up to the next level, spread the circle of gratitude. Get your friends and family in on the act, by creating a gratitude list that you can work on together.

Set everyone the task of writing down five things that they'd like to give thanks for in their lives right now. Once you've done this, set some time aside to share your lists. Be open about the things that matter to you and listen to what others have chosen. You might notice things that you hadn't thought about, which you are also grateful for – add them to your own list so that it grows. The object of this exercise is to make you think and be open to the flow of gratitude in your life.

Next, challenge yourself to think of things outside your circle that you are grateful for, such as the natural world, the animals and birds, the warm weather, the longer days of summer and so on. Set this challenge to your friends and family and see what they come up with, then share your ideas once more. Get into the habit of regularly updating the lists and touching base with those close to you. Talking about the things you all appreciate will attract more of the same and raise your energy vibration so that you'll be able to manifest even more good things.

SHARE THE JOY

SHARE THE JOY

SHARE THE JOY

SHARE THE JOY

SHARE THE JOY

SHARE THE JO

SHARE THE JOY

SHARE THE JOY

The Wider Community

Manifesting doesn't just start and end with you and those close to you. When it comes to shaping your reality, think outside the box and try to manifest things that will benefit others as well yourself. Consider every aspect of your life and all the people you come into contact with, then think about those you don't yet know and how you can build a community spirit.

Why not try manifesting...

- **A tribe:** A group of like-minded friends that you can share your hopes and dreams with.

- **An online community:** A group of friends you can connect with online.

- **Better working relationships:** With those at your work, college or school.

- **A community support network:** A group of people who live in the same area and look out for each other.

- **A mentor:** Someone you can look up to and go to for advice.

- **A happy family dynamic:** Open and loving relationships with family members, even those you don't see often.

- **A spiritual support network:** A group of people who are there for each other and offer spiritual support and guidance.

Further Afield

Engaging with the natural world plays a big part in the manifesting process. To create change and shape the things you want, you need to be connected to your environment. This means working with universal energy in the form of the elements and your surroundings. Immersing yourself in the natural world helps you stay present and also ignites your creativity, which is an essential manifesting tool. It also raises your energy vibration. The more aware you become of your environment, the more you'll hone your intuition and pick up on signs and signals sent to you from the universe. You'll recognize the flow of synchronicity in your life and know exactly when to take action.

MINDFUL WALK

One of the best ways to connect with nature is to take a mindful walk. You can do this anywhere but it helps if you find a green space, somewhere like a park, field or nature reserve.

- Focus on the simple things like the rhythm of your breathing and the sound that your feet make as you walk. Draw in long, deep breaths and, as you exhale, imagine you are releasing anything that might block the manifestation process, such as fears or limiting beliefs.

- Engage all your senses and connect with the environment. Think about what you can see, hear, smell, taste and feel. Pick out specific things. Perhaps you can hear the sound the wind whistling through the trees or smell the aroma of damp earth.

- If you feel your mind wandering, bring your attention back to the pattern of your breathing and remember that every time you breathe in you are raising your energy vibration, and every time you exhale, you are ridding yourself of any limitations.

- As you walk, notice how the world around you develops and grows, and how new things are created in every moment. Draw inspiration from the natural world and know that you too have the power to sow seeds for the future and create all the things you want in your life.

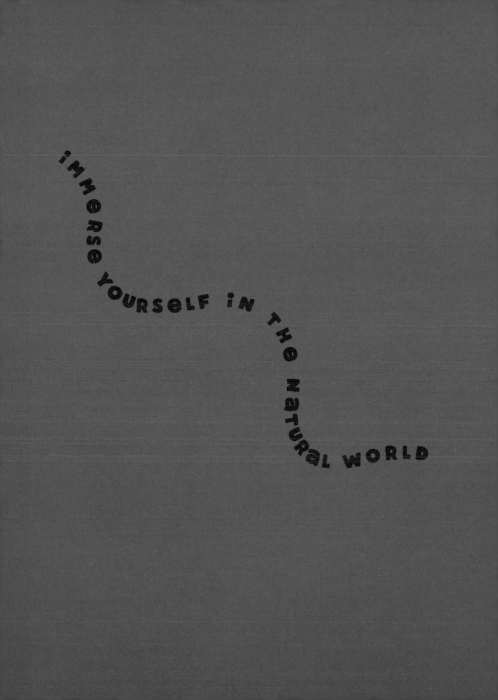

immerse yourself in the natural world

Ten Things You Might Choose to Manifest

Think about breaking down any blocks to manifestation and try some of these options.

1. Problem-solving skills.

2. More energy.

3. Better sleep.

4. More motivation.

5. More confidence.

6. Financial independence.

7. Emotional independence.

8. Honesty and truth in all your relationships.

9. Trust in others.

10. Trust in the universe.

This book gives you the basics to get started on your manifestation journey, but like any expedition what you get out of it depends on what you put in. If you prepare and make sure you are in a positive frame of mind, then every part of the process becomes a joy and you will learn a lot about yourself and the world around you.

Positive thinking is the key to your success. It not only unlocks the door to manifesting glory, it also opens up other avenues. When you get into the habit of focusing on the positive things, this has a knock-on effect on your approach to all aspects of life. You are able to handle challenges effectively and you'll be more open to opportunities. You'll also develop self-confidence and instinctively know when something is right for you.

Manifesting is a wonderful practice that can help boost your self-belief and shape your life in ways you hadn't even imagined. Take it at your own pace and build upon each success, but most importantly enjoy tapping into your creative power. Once you get into the flow, you'll find that things have a habit of evolving perfectly for you at the right time because you are in sync with the universe.

Alison Davies runs workshops at universities throughout the UK, showing academics, students and early years practitioners how stories can be used as tools for teaching and learning. Alison also delivers workshops on the power of narratives and how they can change your life. Alison writes for a wide selection of magazines, including *Take A Break*, *Fate and Fortune*, *Spirit & Destiny*, *You*, *Kindred Spirit*, *Take A Break Pets* and *Woman's Own*. Her features have also appeared in the *Times Education Supplement*, *Daily Mail*, *Daily Express* and *Sunday Express* parenting section, and various commercial magazines.

Managing Director Sarah Lavelle
Commissioning Editor Sarah Thickett
Copy Editor Wendy Hobson
Proofreader Emma Bastow
Designer Alicia House
Illustrator Kelli Laderer
Head of Production Stephen Lang
Production Controller Sabeena Atchia

First published in 2023 by Quadrille,
an imprint of Hardie Grant Publishing
Quadrille
52–54 Southwark Street
London SE1 1UN
quadrille.com

The content of this book is the opinion of the author and is not intended as a substitute for professional advice (financial, medical or otherwise), diagnosis or treatment. Always seek the advice of a qualified health provider with any questions you may have regarding a medical condition. The author and publisher do not assume responsibility for and hereby exclude to the fullest extent possible at law, any and all liability for any loss, damage, injury, illness or loss of life caused by negligence (including incorrect information in this book) or mistakes in the interpretation of the information in this book.

Cataloguing in Publication Data: a catalogue record for this book is available from the British Library.

ISBN 978 1 78713 931 2

Printed in China

MIX
Paper from responsible sources
FSC
www.fsc.org
FSC™ C020056